Return of the Wolf

written by Dan Piparo and Patsy Jensen

illustrated by Constance R. Bergum

McGraw-Hill
School Division

New York   Farmington

In 1986, the United States government began a program to bring wolves back to our wilderness areas. Many people felt this was a good idea. However, many others felt it was a terrible plan.

The people who were furious about the wolves were farmers and ranchers. Years before, almost all of the wolves had been killed by farmers and ranchers who were hunting them.

They hunted wolves because the wolves killed their animals. Wolves had always hunted wild animals in the forest. After the trees in the forests were cut down to make room for farms, the wolves no longer had enough animals to hunt. They went to farms and ranches, where they could find chickens, sheep, and even cattle to eat.

Another reason that people hunted wolves was for their fur.

There are two types of wolves in the United States. They are the gray wolf and the red wolf.

The gray wolf is also called the timber wolf. Its fur can be any color from white to solid black. It lives in wooded areas. A hundred years ago, the gray wolf lived in many parts of the United States. By 1970, the gray wolf only remained in Alaska and Minnesota.

The red wolf, which is smaller than the gray wolf, lives mainly in the South. The red wolf is not really red. Its fur is a blend of brown and black. The red wolf had almost become extinct by 1975. Fortunately, the government started a program to raise red wolves in captivity. In 1986, red wolves were released in North Carolina. By 1990, the situation of the red wolf had improved.

Wolves are social and they live in packs. The pack hunts together, going after animals that are old, weak, or young. In spite of their speed, teeth, and claws, wolves only get their prey about once in every ten tries.

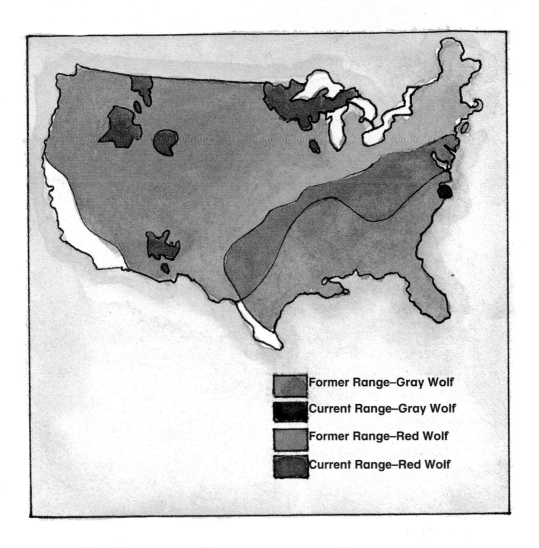

Former Range–Gray Wolf
Current Range–Gray Wolf
Former Range–Red Wolf
Current Range–Red Wolf

Until not too long ago, people were allowed to hunt wolves. In fact, the government used to encourage the hunting of wolves. Today, however, it is against the law to kill wolves.

In 1995, the government brought 29 gray wolves from Canada to the Rocky Mountains. These wolves were placed in two different areas.

A year later, 37 more gray wolves were
brought to the United States from Canada.
Scientists were happy to see that both
groups of wolves had settled in.

Then a wonderful thing happened. Slowly,
packs of wolves from Canada began to travel
on a route to the United States on their own.

Scientists discovered that two litters of wolf pups were born in our country in 1995. Two years later, 20 more litters were born here. The program was a success! There is no longer a need to bring more wolves to the United States. Wildlife experts are delighted that the wolves are thriving. They think that wolves help keep a balance of animals in nature.

Of course, not everyone was happy about the wolves' return. Farmers and ranchers were furious. They were afraid that wolves would begin killing their livestock again.

Only about five sheep are actually killed by wolves each year.

A wildlife group thought of a plan to solve this problem. They collected money to help farmers and ranchers. The money is used to pay farmers and ranchers to replace any animal killed by wolves. This fund of money has helped some people stop worrying about wolves.

Scientists and other people who care
about animals keep track of the wolf
population. They make sure the wolves are
not causing trouble. For example, if a wolf
kills livestock, it is moved to another place.
If it kills livestock a second time, the wolf is
killed. Wildlife experts feel that this is the
best way to be fair to farmers and ranchers.

There are other reasons why some people do not like wolves. In many folktales and fairy tales, wolves are often shown to be bad and dangerous. Sometimes wolves are disguised as people. Or they pace up and down outside a house, threatening to eat the people inside.

For centuries people have told frightening stories about wolves. This is why many people think that wolves hurt humans. The truth is that there have been only two reported wolf attacks on humans in North America. And both are thought to be times where the wolf needed to protect itself.

But some businesses that are near the areas where wolves live do not mind the reputation that wolves have. In fact, they are happy to have wolves around. The wolves help them make money. Can you guess how?

Gray wolves bring more tourists to areas like Yellowstone Park in Wyoming. Red wolves bring people who are interested in wolves to states like Tennessee and North Carolina.

Then hotels, restaurants, stores, and gas stations in these places can make money from the wolf watchers. Some stores even sell T-shirts and coffee mugs with pictures of wolves on them.

Scientists think that having more wolves will bring good changes for other animals and plants where they live. Because the wolves which hunt deer and elk have been gone for so long, some deer and elk herds have become too big. The herds eat all the grass, and then are forced to look for food closer to where people live.

Wolves will kill the weak and old animals in these herds. Then the other deer and elk will have plenty of food. Other animals can also eat the deer and elk that the wolves have killed.

Wolves can solve another problem in nature. The coyote population has grown too big. Wolves are natural enemies of coyotes. Experts think that with more wolves around, there will be fewer coyotes. This will help animals like foxes, which are hunted by coyotes.

It will take time for these changes in animal populations to happen. However, these positive changes have already begun.

The government now protects wolves. There are serious punishments for killing a wolf in the United States. A guilty person might have to go to jail and pay as much as a $100,000 fine!

These punishments show that the government feels it is very important to protect wolves.

But in all parts of the country, wolves
continue to face difficulties. Some farmers
and ranchers are trying to get the laws
that protect wolves taken away. For wolves
to survive, people must have a better
understanding of them. Once people learn
how important wolves are in nature, wolves
will have a better chance of living safely in
the United States for many years to come.